YOUR FIRST CORPORATE JOB *Made Easy*

7 Secrets Guaranteed To Kickstart Your New Career And Help You Avoid Common Mistakes

---

Special <u>FREE</u> Bonus Gift for You
To help you to achieve more success, there are
FREE BONUS RESOURCES for you at:

www.FreeGiftFromDaniela.com

- 3 in-depth training videos on how to excel in corporate

DANIELA NGOUNOU®

Copyright © 2022 Daniela Ngounou, Inc.

ALL RIGHTS RESERVED. No part of this book or its associated ancillary materials may be reproduced or transmitted in any form or by any means, electronic or mechanical, including photocopying, recording, or by any informational storage or retrieval system without permission from the publisher.

'PUBLISHED BY: Daniela Ngounou, Inc.,

DISCLAIMER AND/OR LEGAL NOTICES
While all attempts have been made to verify information provided in this book and its ancillary materials, neither the author or publisher assumes any responsibility for errors, inaccuracies or omissions and is not responsible for any financial loss by customer in any manner. Any slights of people or organizations are unintentional. If advice concerning legal, financial, accounting or related matters is needed, the services of a qualified professional should be sought. This book and its associated ancillary materials, including verbal and written training, is not intended for use as a source of legal, financial or accounting advice. You should be aware of the various laws governing business transactions or other business practices in your particular geographical location.

EARNINGS & INCOME DISCLAIMER
With respect to the reliability, accuracy, timeliness, usefulness, adequacy, completeness, and/ or suitability of information provided in this book, Daniela Ngounou, Daniela Ngounou, Inc., its partners, associates, affiliates, consultants, and/or presenters make no warranties, guarantees, representations, or claims of any kind. Readers' results will vary depending on a number of factors. Any and all claims or representations as to income earnings are not to be considered as average earnings. Testimonials are not representative. This book and all products and services are for educational and informational purposes only. Use caution and see the advice of qualified professionals. Check with your accountant, attorney or professional advisor before acting on this or any information. You agree that Daniela Ngounou and/or Daniela Ngounou, Inc. is not responsible for the success or failure of your personal, business, health or financial decisions relating to any information presented by Daniela Ngounou, Daniela Ngounou, Inc., or company products/services. Earnings potential is entirely dependent on the efforts, skills and application of the individual person.

Any examples, stories, references, or case studies are for illustrative purposes only and should not be interpreted as testimonies and/or examples of what reader and/or consumers can generally expect from the information. No representation in any part of this information, materials and/or seminar training are guarantees or promises for actual performance. Any statements, strategies, concepts, techniques, exercises and ideas in the information, materials and/or seminar training offered are simply opinion or experience, and thus should not be misinterpreted as promises, typical results or guarantees (expressed or implied). The author and publisher (Daniela Ngounou, Daniela Ngounou, Inc. (DN) or any of DN's representatives) shall in no way, under any circumstances, be held liable to any party (or third party) for any direct, indirect, punitive, special, incidental or other consequential damages arising directly or indirectly from any use of books, materials and or seminar trainings, which is provided "as is," and without warranties.

WHAT OTHERS ARE SAYING ABOUT DANIELA AND HER STRATEGIES

"What I loved so much about Daniela was not only her excitement but her being able to translate it to tangible and actionable steps for my audience and how they can show up more powerfully"

~ Caleb Guilliams CEO of Better Wealth, Financial Advising Company

"You were such a blessing and had a great message. I am beyond happy and
grateful for you. It Blessed my soul and I know it blessed many others."

~ Morgan James, Founder of His Daughter's Closet

"Thank you so much Daniela for educating and inspiring me. This will prepare me for my future. Some people including myself are unsure where to start. This was sooo good!"

- Young Professional Workshop Attendee

Thank YOU very much for all you did to make the Girls of Faith event so special. We had so much positive feedback about the event. Having you there really offered a next level experience

~ Alberta Swain, Troop Experience Manager
Girl Scouts of USA

MOTIVATE AND INSPIRE OTHERS!

"Share This Book"

Retail: $24.95

Special Quantity Discounts

5-20 Books	$21.95
21-99 Books	$18.95
100-499 Books	$15.95
500-999 Books	$10.95
1,000+ Books	$8.95

To Place an Order Contact:

daniela@danielangounou.com
www.danielangounou.com

THE IDEAL PROFESSIONAL SPEAKER FOR YOUR NEXT EVENT!

Any organization that wants to develop their people to become "extraordinary," needs to hire Daniela Ngounou for a keynote and/or workshop training!

Meeting Planners' thoughts:

"Daniela was a ball of energy and translates that energy to the audience seamlessly!"

"I will definitely have Daniela back again! The audience loved her!"

TO CONTACT OR BOOK
DANIELA NGOUNOU TO SPEAK:

daniela@danielangounou.com
www.danielangounou.com

THE IDEAL COACH FOR YOU!

If you're ready to overcome challenges, have major breakthroughs and achieve higher levels, then you will love having Daniela Ngounou as your coach!

TO CONTACT
DANIELA NGOUNOU

daniela@danielangounou.com
www.danielangounou.com

Dedication

I want to thank my Lord and savior Jesus Christ for giving me the grace and wisdom to pursue the call He placed in my life with such passion and joy. Every idea, instruction, and lesson I teach in this book is inspired by the Spirit of God and I am honored to serve Him with my life!

> **Charm is deceptive, and beauty does not last; but a woman who fears the Lord will be greatly praised.**
>
> **Proverbs 31:30**

Also, thank you to my 2nd biggest supporters, my family! You have always pushed me to greatness and I am so grateful. My parents raised me to go for my dreams and always believe in myself! I'm doing it mommy and daddy! :)

| Olivier Ngounou | Me | Carelle Ngounou | Diane Wajay | Ornella Bourne | Delphine Ngounou |

Not Pictured: Laurent Wajay & Abdiel Bourne

Table of Contents

Introduction: A Message to You!		**Page #10**
Secret 1:	**You Have Nothing To Prove**	**Page #12**
Secret 2:	**The Winner's Mindset**	**Page #31**
Secret 3:	**Stop Saying Sorry**	**Page #46**
Secret 4:	**Manage Up**	**Page #64**
Secret 5:	**Dealing With A Bad Boss**	**Page #81**
Secret 6:	**Don't Network! Build Relationships**	**Page #91**
Secret 7:	**The Power Of Mentorship**	**Page #100**
BONUS!	**The Unfair Advantage**	**Page #109**
One Last Message!		**Page #112**

A Message to You!

Let me tell you about an amazing free investment you can make towards your future.

Imagine yourself six months to a year from now, living the life you want to live. It can be a car you want to drive, the children you wish to have, the career you want to have, the business you want to run, the amount of money you want to make, the family you want to be surrounded by, or the friends you want to have. Literally, whatever it is that is important to you.

Really place yourself there and feel the emotions of what it would feel like to live that life, and the experience you would have in it. Do a google search if you have to! Just get the image of the important things to you, and imagine yourself experiencing them.

Now that you have stretched your imagination, write about it! Your written word is super important. Because once you write something down, you freeze the idea on paper.

If you are wanting to manifest or experience something in your life, write it in your letter.

You will write this letter in the past tense. Why? It makes you talk about it as if it already happened. This is powerful!

You are going to read this letter every single day! This will make you use the power of spoken words every day to instill and affirm your goals. This will also help you believe that what you are saying is true, and you will begin to work towards those things to see them play out in your life. The Bible instructs us to speak things that are not as though they were (Romans 4:17). Because we live by faith, we have to see things in our imaginations before we see them physically. Reading your letter daily is powerful because it pushes you to walk in a principle that God has already set on the earth from the beginning of time!

As you read this book, I guarantee you will learn things you have never heard before, so adjust your letter accordingly! I am so excited about how this letter, accompanied by the strategies in this book will change your life. I pray in the name of Jesus that every single desire you have will come to pass according to God's will for your life!

"YOUR WORDS ARE POWERFUL"

~ Daniela Ngounou
Founder of The Professionals on Fire Network
www.danielangounou.com

SECRET ONE

You Have NOTHING To Prove!

Stepping into a new role can feel intimidating. You are often thinking of ways to prove to the company that you are worthy of the new role. You probably want to stay on your P's and Q's because you fear messing up and ruining the opportunity. I understand and can relate because it happened to me.

I started my career as a consultant in one of the big 4 accounting firms. Before starting, I repeatedly heard from others that I have to walk into the job proving (to other employees and executives) that I am comfortable working in a cutthroat environment. In addition, I need to follow along with how the team operates so that I don't get in anyone's way.

I was told I was probably not going to enjoy my job because of the long hours, work environment, and culture. I was told that I had to endure all of the hardship because it was my duty to prove myself to the leadership of the firm; especially in the first couple of years of my career.

According to many who advised me, my job was to stay in my lane and go above and beyond what I am asked to do. This means that if I am supposed to be at work at 8:00 am, I am expected to show up earlier and if I am meant to leave at 5:00 pm, I should stay longer. This will surely prove to them that I am a great employee.

Can I let you in on a little secret?

You have nothing to prove! This may be very surprising to you because it is contrary to what most people say to you when you are starting a new career. However, let me explain that you have nothing to prove!. Trust and believe that when you understand this, your career will begin to progress immensely!

The company hired you because they believed in you. You showed them you were worthy of this role before they hired you. The company already has a good feeling that you are perfect for the position they hired you for, that's why they did it!

This discovery often happens during the interview process. The reason why interviews can be so extensive is because companies are looking for a great fit, so they ask relevant questions to determine if you would qualify for the role.

Because of this, you have ALREADY proven that you are fit for your role. Having heard this explanation, I urge you to throw away the "I have something to prove" mindset; that part is already done! If you are already getting paid, you already have the offer and you're walking into your first day at the company! Again I say, YOU HAVE NOTHING TO PROVE!

Let me explain why this is so important. When you are constantly in the "you have something to prove" mindset, you hold yourself back. You'll begin to create a false image in your mind about who you think you are supposed to be, whether or not the company has asked you to be that person.

When you create an image of someone you wish you were in your mind, as opposed to a better version of your current self, you will unfairly compare yourself to that image. It's unfair to yourself because you are creating unrealistic expectations for yourself by comparing yourself to an image that isn't you and is nothing like you. This is a problem. You will only grow into a better version of yourself. You will never grow to be someone else. Therefore if the image in your head is not a better version of yourself, you need to change it!

As long as you do not see yourself as someone perfect for your position, you are always going to want to be like the person you create in your head! You may even hold yourself back from doing things unless you are sure the person in your head would do it.
This is extremely inauthentic. The problem here is that the person in your head is not you. And the longer you compare yourself to someone else (even if it is an image you have created in your mind), you will always fall short.

Why are you setting yourself up to always fall short at the beginning of your career?

You may have heard the phrase "Comparison is the thief of joy".

This is something we deal with in so many areas of life but let's take the example of social media today. I am sure you have compared yourself with something or someone on social media before and you probably didn't feel very good about it afterward right?

When you look at someone you wish you were like or look at something that you wish you had, you start thinking about how you will probably never be like them or look at all of your limitations to try and make sense of why you haven't made it to that level in your life.

Then, you look at how much younger the person is compared to you and start wondering, "Will this ever happen for me?".

This is when worry and fear kick in. Now, instead of leaving the social media page inspired, you leave feeling less than and full of fear because you worry that you will never achieve your goals.

Fear and worry are the only outlets that derive from comparison.

Instead of comparing yourself, stay in the spirit of inspiration!

Let's look at this same example from a different perspective. . You set a goal to get promoted to a senior position in your company. However, you feel as if you have a lot to learn and accomplish in order to be trusted to perform well at that level.
Rather than worrying and being fearful, decide to make a plan for yourself to reach your goal.

Write down all of your strengths (attributes that you are already performing highly at) as well as your weaknesses (Skills that can be improved, which will also contribute to the senior role)). Now that you have this information, utilize social media, blogs, or articles to your advantage. Find people who were once in your shoes and achieved their goal of a promotion.

Furthermore, listen to learn about their journey, struggles, and breakthroughs. In doing this research, you will be grateful when you find someone relatable to you. You may even comment on a post to thank them for sharing their journey.

This will make you so excited to know that you now have the resources to accomplish your goals that you will begin taking action according to the research you have done! Now that you approached social media and other search platforms intentionally with a plan, you will leave inspired and encouraged to achieve your desired goal!

In this example, we see that inspiration comes from gratitude.
A state of inspiration is always better than a state of fear. Understand this: fear does nothing but take your blessings away and honestly, it doesn't feel good at all!

You might be wondering why I just took you through this exercise. The reason is to enlighten you so that you can see the importance of staying far away from fear when beginning your first corporate job.

In addition, comparing yourself to someone else (even if it's "just" the person you created in your mind) will always lead down a path of worry, fear, and anxiety. As long as you try to be the person in your head, you will never come across as an authentic person because it will be apparent that you are trying to be someone that you are not. The best person to be is you. The more authentic you are, the better you show up because you don't have to try to be yourself, you just are. No one can take from you. You are your biggest asset!

Instead of]comparing yourself to an unrealistic image all of the time, keep in mind the inspiring stories that you find instead. This will help you remember two important ideologies:

1. You are not alone.
2. You are working to create your own inspirational story in your career.

Think about it this way; successful people never reach success by trying to be like other people. Successful people reach success by aspiring to outdo themselves until they are the best in their category. They often use other stories or journeys to stay committed, however, their goal is to do better than yesterday, that's it!

"I am not the next Usain Bolt or Michael Phelps, I am the first Simone Biles"

Simone Biles,
Gymnast, 7 Time Olympic Medalist

In this quote, Simone Biles is focused on being the first of her kind, not a copy of someone else. This shows true confidence. When you take your eyes off of others and focus on making yourself better, you can be authentically YOU! And that is the best gift you can give to your employer. Remember, you are amazing, that's why they hired you!

I hope you now understand that you have nothing to prove, and furthermore, why it's important to throw away that mindset! Next, let's focus on what mindset you ought to cultivate instead. It is not a secret that you must perform well and excel in order to keep your job. So, how exactly do you do that?

YOU ADD VALUE

Walk into your new job every day with this thought in mind,
"I am going to add value to my team today."

Adding value simply means to make the team, project, or company better by doing something that makes work easier, more enjoyable, or effective.

Yes, I recognize that you are just starting your career and may not have any idea how you can achieve this. However, it is a lot easier than you think.

Ask yourself some of these questions to brainstorm what adding value may look like:

- Does the team seem disorganized or always have too much to do?
    - You can learn agile methodologies and introduce a project checklist or plan to make things more organized and achievable.

- Would it be useful to send out meeting notes to attendees for important meetings to keep everyone on the same page?
    - Consider taking up this role. This is a great way to stay at the forefront of their minds. Your colleagues will constantly see your name in their emails for important meetings!
    - Don't like taking notes? Still, add value by sending out the action items captured during the meeting with each stakeholder's name next to it. This keeps the team accountable which is helpful for effectiveness!

- What software do you know about that may help your team to perform at a higher level?

  - Depending on your industry, there could be many different answers here. If you are not sure what would be helpful since you are stepping into a new career, data visualization tools are often used across many industries since everyone utilizes and analyzes data in some way, shape, or form.
  - Remember, you don't have to be an expert at any of these. Merely suggesting to use a tool and trying it out to see if it will make the team more efficient will be applauded and can add tremendous value!

- Does the team have a forum that encourages co-workers to get to know each other better and possibly learn from each other?
  - Taking initiative to create the invite and finding a place for the team to meet for a dinner/happy hour is a huge help!
  - Be unashamed of learning! Ask directors and other leaders if they would be open to a Q&A for new hires to better get acclimated to the company and ask questions. This will make you stand out as a leader wanting to learn. Also, it will help you understand your leadership's needs.

- Is there a platform that your company is using that no one knows much about?
    - This is a great way to set yourself apart by becoming the go-to person for something everyone needs! It might require some curiosity and training, but if it is something you are interested in, it is worthwhile.
    - People have created new unique separate roles for themselves by taking initiative on this!

- What else is lacking in your team that may not have been mentioned above? (This doesn't have to be work-related, sometimes teams just need more fun!)
    - There are so many other ways to add value. Think about your company's vision, values, and goals and compare them to what your team does. What is something you can introduce that will help the team grow closer to the company's overall vision and goals?

How can you position yourself to be the answer to that problem? It doesn't have to be in a "major" way. As long as you are looking for ways to create value for either your team or company, you will be ahead of the game.

This will change how you see yourself and the way others perceive you. You're not going to be seen as someone who is trying to be perfect, but instead, you will be seen as the employee who always finds a way to help and make things easier.

Here's something to think about; would you rather be around someone who is constantly trying to prove that they are flawless or around someone constantly trying to make your life easier? Obviously, the person constantly trying to make your life easier right? When your innovative contributions to the team make others' lives easier, you will be remembered as a leader. Leaders take initiative to make things better and more effective. Leaders are people that serve others and are recognized for the value they bring in people's lives.

WiFi is one of those things that is always a value add, and when we cannot access it, everyone is aware and is probably inconvenienced by it. That is why you are more likely to go to a coffee shop that has WiFi and happily buy coffee and snacks because you recognize the value and convenience you are receiving. You will be able to sit on nice chairs, work in peace, and use the WiFi; that is worth a 5 dollar drink!

If you are trying to work on an assignment that requires you to be on the internet, you probably won't consider going to work anywhere that does not have WiFi. So in this case, WiFi is a value add because it makes working remotely more convenient for you.

Did you catch that? Just like you happily spend money in coffee shops that provide a great environment and WiFi, your company will happily give you salary increases and promote you when you add value to them or their employees.

If you adopt this thought process, you will begin to see many ways you can add value and when you start implementing it in your career, you will excel very quickly. This is because your directors, managers, co-workers, and clients will recognize you as someone who betters the team! Therefore, they will always want you around and they won't have a problem incentivizing you to stay!

Let me share a testimony that came about in my career when I implemented these strategies.

As a consultant, I was assigned to a project and the goal was to implement a technology to make their reporting faster and more automated.

As a new associate on the project, I wanted a different experience than my previous project. I realized that trying to prove that I was good enough didn't work. It always made me second guess myself, overthink, and constantly feel less than. I wanted people to get to know me for who I truly was. So when I got a new client, I saw it as an opportunity to change my approach.

I started by bringing my "whole" self to work. I let my personality shine! Even when I gave a presentation to stakeholders! I wanted people to know the authentic Daniela. I started saying "Praise the Lord " when I heard some good news, which is something I do regularly.

However, I never said it around colleagues previously because I did not want to be judged. Being myself allowed me to make great relationships. Both on my team as well as with the client. This helped me look forward to work because I did not have to be someone I wasn't!

I also began looking for ways to add value. After some thought, I observed that we were using excel to report on certain metrics and it was slowing down our progress as a team! The models were pretty complex so it was challenging for my manager to update them with excel.

Because I had some familiarity with Tableau, I used it to create a replica of the report that we had in excel. I then showed it to my manager and asked if we could use Tableau going forward and share it with the client. My manager was pleased with me! I took the initiative on something that was consuming a lot of time and found an innovative solution.

Using Tableau for the report made it easier to understand because it is a visual tool. It also made the report much faster to compile. Once we showed the client, they were very happy with it and even considered buying licenses for Tableau because it made their reporting that much faster!

When it came time to downsize the team because the project work was slowing down, the client chose to keep me on the team out of 4 other consultants. Why? I was adding value to them and they wanted to keep me around due to my positive attitude and bubbly personality.

I was never trying to prove to anyone that I was better during my time with that client. I was never trying to be like anyone else on the project. I was focused on being myself and using my interest/skills to make the team work better and faster.

This will be your story as well if you choose to let go of the mindset of having something to prove and focus on being authentic and adding value. When you do that, you will be the only person in your category, making you unique and irreplaceable.

"If Your Presence doesn't add value, your absence won't make a difference"

Zero Dean

Reflection and Action Steps

What have you learned in this chapter?

How do you plan on implementing it?

SECRET
TWO

The Winner's Mindset

One day, I walked into the office and met an executive that would help with our project for some time. For some reason, I did not hit it off with him. I was very amiable to him like I was to everyone else on the team but we just didn't seem to click, I wasn't sure why. I did not let it bother me, however. I continued about my work and everything else I was doing.

As he took on more responsibility on the team, I started being heavily involved in his meetings and the work he was supporting.

Unfortunately, however, every time I suggested something or asked him a question, he ignored me. Yes, you read that right – he flat out ignored me multiple times. On different occasions and days. This was concerning, considering that he was a very important executive on the project and had a say in my promotional conversations.

You are probably wondering what I did about it at this point. Well, I didn't complain to him or make a big deal about it. Instead, I kept approaching him, doing the work I was assigned and kept letting my personality shine.

Why? Because I was not going to allow someone else's attitude to affect my performance or potential for growth.

I dedicated myself to starting my career with a winner's mindset and nothing, I mean nothing, was going to stop my success.

When you make up your mind to be headstrong no matter what comes up, you will always see a victory. Long story short, that executive ended up being a great mentor of mine and helped me grow exponentially! Why? I added value. He had no choice but to recognize that I was extremely useful to the team. Because of the mindset I had, I chose to have a great attitude no matter how he was treating me. I chose to forgive quickly when he decided to start building a better relationship with me. Honestly, if I didn't choose to have a positive mindset toward the situation, I would have missed out on a great mentor! After he recognized my value, I could have held a grudge and would have rejected the blessings that came with being under his mentorship.

There is a big part of the story missing but I will talk more about that in the bonus chapter of this book – don't miss it!

Right now we are focused on mindset. It is one of the biggest secrets to a great experience in a corporate setting.

Let's have a look at the definition of the word mindset.

Mindset; the established set of attitudes held by someone.

Notice that the definition of mindset places responsibility on you to establish a set of attitudes you will live by. This shows that it is up to you to decide what kind of attitudes you want to have and hold at any moment of your life.

In the story I shared earlier about a difficult work experience, I mentioned something that will help you tremendously: "Instead, I kept approaching him, doing the work I was assigned, and kept letting my personality shine." I decided to have a positive attitude towards anyone at any time, no matter how I was treated in the workplace.

If I chose to get bogged down and discouraged instead of maintaining my positivity, the situation probably could have gotten worse because I would have not been able to show up to work authentically. I most likely would have tried to prove that I was worthy of being heard, and we talked about the effects of that last chapter.

The reality is that what you choose to think about carries a lot of power. Your mind is very powerful. You see, God made us in a way that gives us the power to control what happens in our lives and it all starts with our thoughts.

This is a law he placed on the earth. People often refer to it as the law of attraction. It is just a fancy way to say that your reality is created by your thoughts. The more you focus on an image in your mind, the faster the image will actualize itself physically. You can experience major breakthroughs in your life by choosing to only think positively and expecting the things that you want to manifest.

It is not magic, it is simply utilizing the power of the mind and reaping its benefits. The mindset you chose to have can literally make or break your career or on a grander scheme, your life.

No wonder why Paul says:

"Finally, brothers and sisters, whatever is true, whatever is noble, whatever is right, whatever is pure, whatever is lovely, whatever is admirable—if anything is excellent or praiseworthy—think about such things."
Philippians 4:8

Your mind is your creation station. You can choose to create something completely undesirable in it every day, or you can use it to create a life and career you love.

So how do you cultivate a winner's mindset? Let's walk through some strategies you should implement from today!

1. Watch your mouth.

Just like your mind, your mouth is a very powerful instrument for your success. The power of your words can run your life. If you think about it, you have become today what you spoke about yourself in your past. Think about the way you used to talk about yourself and the things you always claimed, are those things true today?

When you do this exercise, I am sure you will be surprised about the number of things that you used to say that have come to pass or are on their way to becoming real in your life (good and bad), I certainly was!

This goes to show that however you speak about yourself and whatever you said you're going to be in the past, you start being those things because you spoke about it so much. Again, this isn't magic! It is the way God made us, after his image. Think about it.

God made the world by speaking words. So of course it makes sense that if we are made by his image, our words also create realities!

Have you ever heard of Dr. Emoto's experiment with rice?

The premise of the experiment is that the words you say and the thoughts you think have an energy that can physically manifest over time. In Dr. Emoto's original experiment, he found that, after 30 days, the rice that he spoke kind words to remained mostly white, while the rice that he spoke negatively to, turned moldy, providing physical evidence of the power of words.

How many times have you called yourself an idiot or stupid thinking that you were being humble in front of others? I challenge you to put an end to that today. Your words have power, and your body listens to the words you tell it and begins to act accordingly. It may not be as fast a process as it was with the rice, however, if you don't stop speaking like that to yourself, those words will eventually manifest. Again, it's not magic, it's just how we were created!

Have you ever noticed that when you complain about being annoyed over and over again you stay annoyed and get annoyed more often? When you are working on something difficult at work, don't dwell and complain about how difficult it is. Say something like " I am taking my time to figure this out" instead of "I am so confused, this doesn't make any sense." The words that you speak tell your mind what attitude to have and if you don't break the cycle, you will be frustrated far too often.

This knowledge will cause a breakthrough in your career. Oftentimes you say bad things about yourself to "humble" yourself around others, but it is affecting your reality little by little. You do not have to bash yourself to be humble. Bashing yourself is not humility, it is insecurity.

Transform your mind by taking your words more seriously and finding more positive ways to talk about yourself. As long as you are speaking negatively, it will be very hard to maintain a positive mindset. When you choose to speak positively about all aspects of your life, you will see it positively affect your life and career in a major way.

A great way to start implementing positive speaking is through affirmations. An affirmation is a statement that you say to yourself every day to help reprogram your mind about how you ought to think and who you are. You are re-teaching yourself about who you really are.

For example, if you want to be more confident, you can affirm yourself every day by saying "I am confident." The more you say that to yourself, the more you will think of ways to build your confidence and take steps until you have reached your goals.

It's the same reason why when you learn something new, you hear about it so much more right after. What you focus on also focuses on you. So if you are affirming to yourself that you are confident, you will begin to easily find resources and ideas about how to make it a reality.

Here are some great affirmations you can use for your first job in a corporation. Pick a couple of them and begin to say them daily!

- I am an amazing professional.
- I add value to everyone I work with.
- I am productive and efficient with my time.
- My skills are valuable and appreciated.
- I show up authentically every day.
- I am unashamed of who I am.
- I am never afraid to ask for help.
- I do all things with confidence.
- If someone does not like me, it has nothing to do with me.
- I am confident and I believe in myself.
- Every day, in every way, I'm getting better and better.
- My work is important, and so am I.
- I am a creative and competent individual.
- I am a person of worth.
- Every mistake and setback I encounter is an opportunity to learn and grow.
- My work ethic is strong and productive.
- My work makes a difference to the world around me.

Chose to Speak INTO your life, not AGAINST it
Daniela Ngounou

2. Watch who you hang around

You may think it has nothing to do with your career, but it actually has a huge impact on your success. Think about the shows that you watch, the people that you follow on social media, and even more importantly, your friend group!

Start taking note of how you feel after watching a certain show or hanging around a certain person. If you don't leave them feeling inspired or fulfilled in some type of way, it probably is not the best environment for you.

Think about your friend group. What do you often spend your time talking about? Are they pursuing a career and taking steps towards self-development or are they "going with the flow" of life? If you want to be successful, it is very important that you surround yourself with those who are on their way, as well as some people who are already there. I am sure you have heard of the phrase:

"Show me your friends and I'll show you your future."

You become like the people who you hang out with. You may not think so, but your friends influence the kind of music you listen to, the places you go, the decisions you make, and how you go about life in general.

You probably have a couple of friends who you think "oh, I'm not like them." You can have the best character and be a great person with amazing goals, but the crowd that you surround yourself with can change that without you even realizing it because it will feel natural.

If you are the only person in your friend group who has big goals and vision, it will be a lot harder to accomplish them, especially if you hang out with them often.

Your friends don't have to be in the same industry as you. They don't even have to have the same interests as you. As long as they are working towards their big goal or vision, it will motivate you to do the same for yourself.

Friends make things look achievable and attainable because you can relate to them. If you follow someone on social media who explains to you how they made their first million, you may feel inspired; however, it may still be difficult to relate to them just because you don't know them personally. If a friend that you hang out with tells you they made their first million, you are going to feel empowered to do the same because the friend is much more relatable to you, making the goal seem much more achievable and attainable.

Again, surround yourself with those who inspire you and those with similar goals in life, because chances are, if you are around them enough, you'll pick things up from them. Surround yourself with people who have a positive outlook on life and will uplift you in the times you need encouragement.

Yes, we are still talking about the mind. Because as you can see there are many different factors that affect the mind.

"Every day, stand guard at the door of your mind, and you alone decide what thoughts and beliefs you let into your life." Will you give in to the temptation to think negatively and stagnate – and then blame others when you don't reach your goals? Or will you guard your mind and only allow in positive thinking that propels you toward the life you dream of? It's up to you."

Jim Ron

www.danielangounou.com

Reflection and Action Steps

What have you learned in this chapter?
How do you plan on implementing it?

_____
_____
_____
_____
_____
_____
_____
_____
_____
_____
_____
_____
_____
_____
_____

SECRET
THREE

Stop Saying Sorry

The average person is predicted to say "I'm sorry" 2.3 million times in a lifetime. That would be:
- 23,000 times a year (assuming a lifetime is 100 in this example)
- 1,917 times in one month
- 63 times in one single day

Let me break this down in a different way so you can see how alarming this is. Let's say it takes 2 seconds to say the words "I'm sorry". Let's disregard the fact that most people say it and it comes with a long explanation of what they should have done instead.

- That would be 4.6 million seconds of saying sorry in a lifetime
- 76,666 minutes of saying sorry in a lifetime
- 1,277 hours of saying sorry in a lifetime
- 53 days of saying sorry in a lifetime
- 1.7 months of saying sorry in a lifetime

That's a lot of time to be sorry! If you continue to say sorry at the average rate that others do in a lifetime, you will end up spending almost two months of your lifetime saying "I am sorry."

Unfortunately, these statistics are even worse for women. Women are reported to say sorry 25% more than men! This makes the statistics above considerably worse if you are a woman.

So, if you say this word so much, what does it even mean? The definition(s) of sorry, per Google is:

🔊 **sor·ry**
/ˈsärē,ˈsôrē/
adjective

1. Feeling distressed, especially through sympathy with someone else's misfortune:
    a. Feeling regret or penitence:
    b. Regret: feel sad, repentant, or disappointed over something that has happened or been done, especially a loss or missed opportunity
2. Penitence: the action of feeling or showing sorrow and regret for having done wrong; repentance
    a. In a poor or pitiful state or condition
3. Having read those definitions, please think about the number of things you usually say sorry for. Are you really feeling distressed or in a pitiful state or are you just using the word to excuse yourself for something minor?

You most likely say sorry in place of "excuse me" because it just feels normal. Well, you are reading this book because you want to be different and separate from those around you, so I am here to tell you that you need to stop saying sorry.

The phrase " I am sorry" is not necessarily a bad thing to say or a bad way to express yourself, you simply need to start using it properly.

According to the definitions of sorry, it seems more appropriate to use the phrase to show sympathy for someone else's situation, or when you are (truly) in a state of deep remorse or sadness over something. If you are using the phrase "I am sorry" but you aren't feeling anything related to the definition, you are using it incorrectly!

Note that the word "sorry" is an adjective, not a verb. That means when you say "I am sorry" you are describing yourself at the moment, not "doing" anything because the word is an adjective.

The survey above also found that 43% of people admit that they regularly apologize when OTHER people do something wrong to them. For example, when someone bumps into you in the hallway, and even though it wasn't your fault, you say "I'm sorry." So really you are saying "I am in a state of deep sadness or distress that you just bumped into me." Sounds obnoxious, doesn't it?

This is very important in order to thrive in a corporation because it highly affects how others perceive you. Here is what happens when you overuse the word "Sorry."

1. **People lose respect for you**

In her book "The Power of an Apology," Beverly Engel says that over apologizing isn't so different from over-complimenting. You may think that you're displaying yourself as a nice and humble person, but in reality, you are sending the message that you lack confidence. She observes that

"It can even give a certain kind of person permission to treat you poorly, or even abuse you."

I most definitely agree with Beverly Engel on this and have seen the effect of this in my career before I stopped overusing the word sorry.

Have you ever noticed that people who are confident or perceived as confident rarely say "sorry" or apologize for their actions?

Part of being confident is believing that you are great at what you do while giving yourself room for error. A confident person does not have to be someone who has no flaws. Instead, they are aware of their strengths and do not look at their flaws as a disadvantage or hindrance, but as an opportunity to collaborate and uplift others – more on how to do this later.

That is why a confident person rarely says "sorry." The more highly you think of yourself, the less you will feel distressed or sad about mistakes or errors you make because you will see them as opportunities to collaborate with other people!

Did you catch that? This is a very important lesson about self image that will upgrade your confidence level dramatically. When you start building your confidence in the workplace, you will find fewer reasons to explain yourself or apologize because you will believe that you are doing the correct things and can justify or stand by it if something were to come up.

I am not talking about being arguable and defensive. Sometimes you can do the right thing the right way and because of time or other factors of the project, something that was not planned and out of your control can come up.

This doesn't make it your fault. It's part of the reason you have a job because things come up and we are there to handle them. There is no need to apologize when something comes up and it changes your work timeline or causes you not to make a deadline. These things happen.

Choosing not to apologize may also have psychological benefits. According to a study published in The European Journal of Social Psychology, researchers found that participants who refused to express remorse showed signs of "greater self-esteem, increased feelings of power (or control) and integrity."
I am not telling you to become an insensitive person who never apologizes. I am simply suggesting to you that you may be overusing the phrase "I'm sorry" and showing you that it might be causing you to be less confident and making others perceive you as such.

2. It lessens the impact of future apologies

Another effect of overusing the phrase "I'm sorry" is that it makes it less effective. It is the same idea as "The Boy Who Cried Wolf." When you say sorry for every little thing, it will carry less weight later on. So when you are in a situation that warrants a sincere apology, the person receiving the apology may not understand how you feel because they hear it from you every day.

If the phrase "I'm sorry" becomes part of your everyday language, it will be interchangeable with other expressions like "um" or "wow" and people may think that it is just part of how you express yourself – don't let that happen because it can hinder your career growth.

A lack of intentionality is a quick way to lose respect from others. "I am sorry" should never be something you say on autopilot, it should be said intentionally and on purpose. Growing a habit to become intentional in your speech will grow your self-esteem and create mutual respect between you and those you work with.

3. It may hinder your career

Do not be the sorry new hire. If you are, it may be detrimental to your career growth. If you become known as someone who is always sorry and is constantly trying to explain a mistake, it may repel others from wanting to work with you.

If you are constantly in distress about something you did at work, it is perceived that you are still at a level that needs a lot of hand-holding and guidance.

Notice I used the word perceived. I am not suggesting that you are going to walk into work on your first day and have all of the confidence in the world. However, people will form an opinion about you depending on how you present yourself by the way you speak and act. You should learn how to do these things earlier on in your career so that career development happens naturally for you.

Most professionals do not understand this and will struggle for promotions due to the lack of this knowledge. Oftentimes, they will have the experience needed and the ability to do the work. However, the way that they present themselves in conversations and body language can tell a different story.

Think about it, would you trust a manager who overuses the word sorry to run your company? I certainly wouldn't. I would want someone who is more sure of themselves because it would reflect the message that my company is self-sufficient and able.

To excel and be set apart in your first corporate job, let go of the idea that overusing the word "sorry" just shows that you're sympathetic to other people. This is not about women having to change to be more like men to gain respect. The word sorry is simply being used incorrectly, and both men and women should stop abusing the word, especially if they are trying to grow in their role.

As a woman in corporate, I used to overuse "sorry" because I felt it was a great way to let people know I care and that I wanted to do better, especially being in a male-dominated workplace. However, I came to realize that it was only keeping me at a place where I wasn't easily trusted. In case you are wondering, I got the same results when overusing the word "sorry" around women at work as well.

Overusing the word "sorry" has the same effects on both women and men in the workplace. Women do not react differently toward a person who overuses the word. However, women, as of today, are more likely to say it, which is not helpful when trying to step into higher level roles.

"I am sorry" vs. "I apologize"

We already covered the meaning of the word sorry. Now, let's talk about an alternative expression, "I apologize."
According to Google, here is the definition of apologize.

a·pol·o·gize
/əˈpäləˌjīz/
verb

To express regret for something that one has done wrong.

We can see here that the word "apologize" is a verb, not an adjective like the word "sorry." This means that if you choose to use it, you are actually "doing" something as opposed to sharing your emotions about a particular situation.

Looking at its definition, I tend to resonate with apologizing more, especially when thinking about the workplace environment. It is very possible for me to be regretful about a mistake or an action and apologize for it.

Here is a great rule of thumb:

Apologize for the actions that you sincerely believe you have done wrong, and express being sorry in situations you sincerely feel sad about something that happened, regardless if it was your fault or someone else's.

What can you say instead?

Earlier in this chapter, you learned that a confident person is aware of their strengths and does not look at their flaws as a disadvantage or hindrance, but as an opportunity to collaborate and uplift others. If you were wondering how you can uplift others with your flaws, get ready to be blown away!

People love to be celebrated. Weddings, birthdays, and anniversaries are times when people spend the most money because it is their time to be lifted, appreciated, and loved.

Knowing this, strive to celebrate people when you get a chance. It shows that you care and are not self-centered. For example, instead of being sorry for being late, thank the person waiting for you for their patience or understanding. Doing this will take the attention away from you, celebrate the other person for their kindness, and allow you to be confident all at the same time!

Gratitude for others is a great way to handle your flaws or mistakes without putting yourself down. Gratitude is the best way to start everything because it sets the mood for positivity and appreciation.

Every time you get the urge to say

sorry, think about ways that you can show gratitude instead. This will make others appreciate your appreciation for them as well as perceive you as a confident and competent person.

Think about it, when someone thanks you for your understanding or patience, you assume that they probably had something going on before they met with you right?

Whether it is gratitude to God for a new day or gratitude to your manager for fixing a mistake you made, it will set the mood for a great day/experience.

There are many different situations when you may feel obligated to say sorry. Here is a list of suggestions about what to say instead when approached with a temptation to say sorry or apologize when it isn't really necessary.

Stop Saying Sorry, Say This Instead:

- When joining a meeting late
    - Thank you for your patience!
- When joining a happy hour late
    - Thanks for waiting for me! What appetizers have we ordered?
- When someone catches your mistake and calls it out during a meeting
    - Thanks for calling that out! I will make that change/update as soon as I can
    - Thanks for catching that!
- When your manager fixes a mistake that you made
    - Thank you for showing me the correct way, this is very helpful
- When you bump into someone in the hallway by accident
    - Pardon me! Are you okay?
- When someone else bumps into you in the hallway
    - Are you okay?

- When a deadline that you were assigned has to move due to something out of your control or due to something taking you longer to complete.
    - Due to unexpected changes out of our control, the timeline has been changed, unfortunately. Thank you for your patience in getting this project back on track
    - This is taking longer than I hoped because ____. I will keep you updated as I work towards the completion of the assignment. Thank you for your understanding!
- When someone does something for you before you can get to it
    - Thanks for getting to that, that was very helpful!
        - If this happens, know that you are not lazy, disqualified, or dumb
- If you were asked to do a task but cannot figure it out and have tried your best
    - After spending some time to figure this out, your expertise would be helpful. Can we schedule some time to talk through it? I would appreciate your thoughts on this.

- When someone is trying to walk past you and you are in the way
  - Let me… clear your path, get out of your way, make some space, or whatever phrase fits your fancy
- When you are trying to walk past someone and they are in your way
  - Excuse me, I am going this way (point), thank you
  - Pardon me to you (Left or right), thank you

When it is okay (and recommended) to apologize…

…by using the phrase "I am Sorry…"

- When a coworker experiences a loss
- When you spill coffee on someone's shirt (or anything dramatic like that)
- When you completely forget to complete a major assignment that affects the whole team

…by saying "I apologize…"

- When you forget to send an email and send it later than expected
- When you make someone feel uncomfortable without being aware
- When you cannot replace your apology with a statement of gratitude

So do not throw away your confidence; it will be richly rewarded.

Hebrews 10:35

Reflection and Action Steps

What have you learned in this chapter?

How do you plan on implementing it?

_____

_____

_____

_____

_____

_____

_____

_____

_____

_____

_____

_____

_____

_____

_____

_____

_____

_____

SECRET
FOUR

Manage UP

During my 2nd year of consulting, I realized that while I was doing well, I didn't stand out. I wanted to learn to be the best at what I do so I started looking for answers. My goal was to get the highest rating for my performance evaluation.

As I talked about in previous chapters, I started working on my confidence, mindset, and words. As I gained confidence in myself, I started to be more upfront about what I wanted. Little did I know this would change my career forever!

During my feedback meeting with my managers and director, I told them that I was looking to get the highest performance rating for the next performance year. I also asked them what I should be doing now to perform at that level. During the meeting with my manager, she walked me through what I could do better according to my previous work with her and gave me great pointers on how to go about it.

The meeting I had with one of my directors at the time really impacted me. He gave me a tip that truly changed my career and I am so grateful for it. He told me that I needed to manage my career and not let anyone else do it for me. He said that I had done well by being upfront with him by telling him that I wanted to be given the highest performance rating and that I need to continue to tell EVERYONE the same.

By everyone, he was talking specifically about other directors, senior managers, and partners because they are the group of people who would be in the performance meetings.

First, I was surprised and intimidated by the idea of doing that because I didn't feel like I had a good enough relationship with other higher-level executives to do this. When I expressed that concern to him, he told me that being direct and asking, even if it feels uncomfortable, is what most people don't do, and that is why they don't get what they want. This happens with most new hires and women at work, he said.

He continued by saying the people who get promoted and rated highly for performance aren't necessarily those who do the best work, it is the ones who position themselves the best way.

Even if you are scared to have conversations with these higher-level executives, it is better to do it anyway, they understand what you are doing because they were once there. Everyone likes a go-getter that doesn't let their emotions get in the way, it means they are a self-starter. Anyone who goes out of their way to be a leader in their career will be better off than the person who doesn't.

From there, he instructed me to go and schedule a call with as many high level executives as I could and have a chat with them to tell them what my goals were for the next year.

When I asked him what I should talk about in these meetings, he told me to get in the habit of TELLING and not ASKING. He explained that higher level executives don't get the chance to work with associates on a day to day basis. So instead of asking them what they think, he said that in order to secure a high rating, I should tell them how I am adding value to the work I am currently supporting and what skills and experience I am going to gain throughout the rest of the year.

Either way, he said, they will tell you where they think you are as far as performance but your only job is to make sure they are aware of all of the accomplishments you have made, and are going to make, throughout the year. Lastly, he said, I have to give them the reason they should advocate for me and tell them to because that will put me in control of my career trajectory.

This conversation with my manager changed my career forever!

I went ahead and followed all of his directions throughout the year. Although it was intimidating, I met with partners, directors, and senior managers and told them about my plans and my accomplishments. I had constant feedback meetings with my manager to make sure I had an idea of my growth from her perspective and challenged myself to add value to my team.

As the performance year went by, I updated executives about my accomplishments and skills and kept my relationships with them, and thanked them for being willing to advocate for me.

When it was time for the performance ratings to be announced, I was rated at the highest performance rating, just as I wanted!

One of the most valuable lessons that I learned throughout that season of my career is that I need to have control over my career and tell people what I want!

Take Control of Your Career, No one else will do it for you!

I hope you see the power of controlling your career through this story. A lot of times, people don't get what they deserve in their career because they never ask or they don't take the initiative to make it happen for themselves.

You don't have to be part of that statistic, however. With the strategies in this book, you are going to flourish early on in your career and I am so excited to be part of the journey!

So, what exactly is managing up?

The Harvard Business Review defines managing up as, "Being the most effective employee you can be, creating value for your boss and your company."

I want to add to this definition. Managing up also includes taking the lead in your career to get the best experience in your role. This does not mean you have a bad or a good manager, it just means that you are not leaving your career goals in someone else's hands. Also, managing up also has to do with providing your manager feedback as well. This might sound weird because your manager is your boss, however, this will help you gain management skills as well. After all, for you to work well with your manager, you both have to be aware of how you communicate best. It is not a one-way street.

Your opinions matter!
How can you implement managing up at work?

Putting your career into your own hands!

No one else will advocate for you better than God and yourself! You have to be willing to take the proper steps to advocate for yourself.

One of the first things you should do in any new role is to have conversations with your manager, directors, and partners to set expectations. Even if you will never have a work meeting or work with any of them, still schedule a meeting with them to set your expectations. This will make you stand out and will allow you to build relationships that will advocate for you in the future. Think about it like making an investment in your career development.

Your objective for these meetings is for them to know exactly where you see yourself a year from now at the company and what you plan to do in order to attain this goal. Make sure to ask them for their feedback on your plan and they will surely give you additional thoughts on it.

Also, you want to ask them about the company's promotion structure and growth framework.

Every company works differently so make sure you know how often they have performance reviews, what metrics they use to measure performance, and what their expectations are from you as well.

Additionally, make sure to end the conversation by asking about their work and what they do daily. Oftentimes new hires do not get an overview of the "big vision" that the company wants to accomplish. When you ask them about their work you will get some insight into it and if you think of any ways you can add value, even if it's just an idea, make sure to throw it out there, especially if it is around your area of interest.

It's always good to ask them if there is anything you can help them with. However, make sure that they are aware of what you currently have on your plate and that you are not putting yourself over capacity. You do not have to work for more than what you are paid for!

Although this may be uncomfortable at first, it is the best thing you can do to ensure success. This is because you will become top of mind to them during the year and they will want to follow up with you because you will have created a relationship with them. In addition, higher level executives love ambitious new hires who want to add value and make a great impact at the company.

If you are worried about being seen as needy, rebuke that thought! Remember, the reason why people don't get what they want is that they don't ask or say anything.

Taking these steps will allow you to make a plan with the right target because you will be working towards a goal that has been communicated and defined. This will help your confidence and you will work intentionally because of the guidance you received from upper management.

Ask for feedback

Asking for feedback is very important to know your manager's thoughts about your performance as the year goes by. Make it a habit to ask for real-time feedback after you hand in an assignment, give a presentation, or complete a task that was asked of you.

It is important to ask for both good and constructive feedback so that you have an idea of the things you should keep doing as well as what you need to work on or stop doing. Make it a habit to ask for feedback so it becomes a routine for you and your manager. Constant feedback permits you to perform at your best every day and challenges you to grow professionally.
Receiving feedback is great to help your growth,

and it is also extremely vital because it makes your manager analyze your performance frequently which makes him or her realize how much you are growing throughout the year. It's like planting seeds in your manager's head about how good you are doing. This will force them to recognize you for your efforts later on!

This way, you are making their jobs a lot easier because honestly, managers have a lot more on their plates on top of managing you and helping you grow. The more you take ownership of your progress, the easier it is for your manager.

Always remember that at the end of the day, everyone has a job and they have a personal life, no matter how much responsibility they have at work. Your manager has a social life, a family life, hobbies, vacation plans, other passions, and so much more just like you do!

Don't expect them to chase you to tell you how you did in your presentation. Don't take it personally but they may not be thinking about it because of all the other things that may be floating around in their head. This doesn't mean that they are bad managers or that you are a bad employee. It could be as simple as they forgot. So take control and ask! Help them help you! This will make them excited to help you grow even more!

When the time comes to review your performance for evaluations, it will be very easy for you to have that conversation with them because it will feel normal! No more stress about performance reviews last minute!

Only ask for feedback from managers or seniors that you work with frequently. Remember, you do not want to ASK higher up executives how they think you are doing, you want to TELL them about what you are accomplishing and the value you are creating at your company. Feedback is only reserved for those who see your work frequently because they will be able to see your progress over some time.

For everyone who asks, receives. Everyone who seeks finds. And to everyone who knocks, the door will be opened.

Mathew 7:7- 8

Create a Role For Yourself

Another way to manage up is by creating a role for yourself. What this means is that you want to become the go-to person for something specific on your project or team. This is powerful because you will become top of mind for your team and they will need you, which means you are adding value.

If you are not given anything to handle in the beginning, consider talking to your manager about it and coming up with some ideas you have about things you can handle going forward. I understand you are new to this career, but it doesn't have to be a complex thing by any means! Here is some example of roles you can create for yourself at the beginning of your career:

<u>Send out meeting notes or action items after meetings</u>

- This is one of the easiest things you can do to contribute to the team early on, even if you have no idea what is going on!
- Sending out action items may be better if you are not confident about your notes yet. Just reply all to everyone who attended the meeting and make sure you add the stakeholder names to each bullet point and there you have it you have action items for each meeting!

- Go one step further by capturing these during the meeting and announcing them at the end of the meeting. That way, people will always look to you for action items, giving you a role and adding value to the project!

Create and update a Weekly Project Status on a simple slide
- This may or may not be something that is already done at your company but something that you can do is ask your manager if you can provide status updates. This can be simply done by making bullet points of milestones that you have for the project and also have a red, yellow, and green light for behind, at-risk, and on-track statuses. It's also great to add a date to every milestone to track how close we are getting to the target finish line. Lastly, make a section for the next steps.
- This is especially great if this is not something that is already done. This will put you in a place where people go to you for status on the project!

Set up Meetings

- Electing to set up the meeting often makes your manager's job easier and adds value to the team
- It will also enable you to build relationships easily

Observe your Managers to Learn as well as provide feedback.

You will learn so much by watching your senior level management and taking notes. Don't just be focused on the work they ask you to do. Watch how they interact with their seniors as well.

With this observation, you will find that they run into situations where they don't know what to say either but they find a way to adjust. These skills are very important. Take notes and ask them questions about how they navigate situations you observe so you can grow from their experience as well.

You don't always have to go through something in order to learn. You can learn by observation. Seniors and managers are usually very open about their journeys if you just ask them. Don't wait until you face an issue that you don't know how to solve to figure it out. If you encounter someone who doesn't want to share that's okay, move on – you tried!

I guarantee you will learn so much and be way more prepared for managing when you do this!
Here are some situations that I recommend you take note of how your seniors deal with.

- When the client is unhappy
- When a deadline is missed

- When their boss is around
- When they are unsure what to say
- When they make a mistake or get something wrong
- When they show up late
- How they present slides for a presentation
- When they encounter any difficult situation
- How they provide you with guidance and assign you to work

This exercise is not for you to become just like your manager, it is just for you to observe and possibly gain inspiration. If you find some things that inspire you, highlight them and keep them for future use. If you find something that does not inspire you, throw it away.

You are on your journey to becoming the best (insert your name). This is not for you to compare yourself by any means. But to find inspiration for your career development.

Lastly, be willing to provide feedback to your manager as well. Make sure you do so in a respectful manner. A great way to do this is to say "It would be helpful for me if you could…." or "I perform at my best with …. (the support you would like from your manager)"

Make it a point to manage up. This is a great way to take the lead in your career and make lasting results.

"If you're going to grow, you have to be international"

-Curt Kampmeier

Reflection and Action Steps

What have you learned in this chapter?

How do you plan on implementing it?

SECRET
FIVE

**Dealing With A
Bad Boss**

You may have already heard some horrific stories about bad bosses from mentors, friends, or colleagues. I would love to tell you that you will never have to deal with mean bosses if you keep a positive attitude and apply these strategies. However, I cannot do that because I would be lying to you. Let's look at some statistics from Huffpost about bad bosses.

"Three out of four employees report their boss is the worst and most stressful part of their job."

"50% of employees who don't feel valued by their boss plan to look for another job in the next year."

"American companies spend an estimated $360 billion each year in health care costs as a result of bad bosses."

"Employees with bad managers are among the least productive workers."

"60% of employees working for the U.S. federal government are miserable -- not because of low pay, poor workplace benefits, or insufficient vacation days -- but because they have bad bosses."

"65% of employees say they'd take a new boss over a pay raise."

"37 percent of employees say their boss failed to give credit."

"44 percent of employees say they've been verbally, emotionally, or physically abused by a supervisor in their career."

We can all agree that this is a major problem in corporations today. However, I am an advocate of doing your part by not allowing someone else's character to disrupt or contaminate your own. I have encountered a couple of not-so-good managers in my career, and I've learned some pointers about how to thrive in your role, regardless.

If you are in your new row and you find yourself in this position, understand that this manager does not define you. Regardless of what he or she says, you have already been qualified for this role. Sometimes micromanagers and mean bosses can make you feel like you are not good enough.

Just remember that hurt people hurt people. Unfortunately, people's personal lives also bleed into their professional lives, and oftentimes a mean boss is maybe going through something personally or just never grew up from childhood trauma or habit. If you are in this position right now, use the opportunity for you to grow into a better professional because every time we're faced with a challenge we get the opportunity to become better than we were before.

Even if you never encounter a mean boss, which is certainly my wish for you, you will absolutely encounter a mean coworker, client, or difficult situation that requires you to handle conflict between others.

So how can you deal with a mean boss?

The best way to prepare for a bad boss is to build confidence. You don't want to find out that you are not confident when you are in a place where you need to exercise it.

In previous chapters, we talked about the power of affirmations, positive thinking, and surrounding yourself with those who are going to uplift and inspire you.

The biggest thing that helps my confidence is knowing who I am and what I carry. What I mean by that is that I know that I am a daughter of God and I carry the very spirit of God inside of me. So therefore if I carry the spirit of God who made the whole universe, then I truly believe that I can do all things. I do not look at my qualifications or the things that I have done to gauge how confident I am. I simply am aided by the Holy Spirit, who lives in me.

We also talked about stopping the overuse of the word "sorry". The challenge I gave myself to stop saying sorry really built my confidence because I was looking at ways to show gratitude towards others rather than looking at myself as someone who is sorry or regretful all of the time. This not only helped me be perceived as more confident, but it also helped me believe that I was also confident, which came in handy when dealing with a bad boss later on. I also want to reiterate that reminding yourself that you were hired there for a reason and that you are being paid to be in this position. Use that reindeer to boost your confidence when needed. Do not let this bad boss make you think for a second that you do not deserve this position.

Below are some other suggestions that I believe will help in the season that you are dealing with a bad boss.

Come up with Solutions, Not problems
Always come up with solutions to problems when speaking with them. There will always be a time when something goes wrong at work and you will need to talk to your boss or your manager concerning the issue. At this time, it is best to bring one or two solutions that you suggest would help the situation instead of just bringing up the problem to them. This will allow them to see that you are a problem solver and that you think ahead. Whether or not they accept the

solutions that you bring, they will not be able to say that you are a bad employee because you are constantly trying to bring a solution to the team to add value.

You may be thinking that I'm talking about "performing above and beyond what you are expected to do." While I am a complete advocate of performing at your best at work, I am not an advocate of doing more than what you are paid to do. Therefore, I am not suggesting that you perform above capacity or above your pay. All that I'm suggesting for you to do is to be a problem solver and someone who is a forward thinker.

Keep a Record of Your Achievements

This is something that you should be doing whether or not you have a bad boss. But it comes in handy if your boss will not give you credit for what you have done or attempts to minimize the work that you have already done. Make sure you're keeping track of every single accomplishment that you make throughout the work of the project. Also document any positive feedback you receive from clients or higher levels of management. This will allow you to advocate for yourself whenever your boss will not do it for you.

When you are documenting your progress make sure you have the milestone, date, and any feedback that you received from that accomplishment. Unfortunately, a lot of bad bosses may try to claim that these things did not happen which is why I suggest that you date it and even add any screenshots that you can as well. You can easily do this on a notepad or OneNote. Wherever it is, make sure you can easily access it and be able to refer to it at a later date.

Don't Feed Into Their Negativity

You may find yourself in situations where you are extremely unhappy or want to complain because of the bad environment at work with your manager. In these times it is very important to cling to your positive mindset and decide not to let it affect you. A great way to combat this is to take some time to meditate and focus on what makes you happy. You can do this by taking steps away from your desk at different times of the day to get back into your place of peace to come back stronger.

Speak Up!

If the situation does not get any better and you still have some concerns, definitely speak up. If you have a good relationship with someone else in the company that has a senior role you can get some advice from them or you can go to HR and seek advice about how to deal with this manager. If someone is being extremely inappropriate towards you, please don't try to protect their job. We are all adults and we all understand the consequences of being inappropriate, especially in a work environment. Speak up so that someone else will not have to go through what you're going through, especially if it is causing you danger or harm in any way.

Fight Back!

There is one way that you can fight back against a bad manager that is quite effective as well. This is something that I did in my career journey and it absolutely changed the relationship I had with my manager and turned things around for me. I'll explain more about that in the bonus chapter. Make sure you don't miss it!

Never pay back evil with more evil. Do things in such a way that everyone can see you are honorable. Do all that you can to live in peace with everyone.

Romans 12: 17-21

Reflection and Action Steps

What have you learned in this chapter?
How do you plan on implementing it?

_____
_____
_____
_____
_____
_____
_____
_____
_____
_____
_____
_____
_____
_____
_____
_____
_____
_____
_____

SECRET SIX

Don't Network! Build Relationships

Have you ever been to a networking event and felt like you were being completely fake because you had to force a smile and a handshake with everyone you met? You have probably walked up to someone before with full intentions of getting to know them but because you had in your mind that you were networking you only asked them specific questions about their jobs and avoided anything "unprofessional."

You may have even struggled with what to say because there are only so many small talk conversations that you could think of that were appropriate for networking so you ended up asking about what they do for work, getting their business card, and walking away. Does that sound familiar to you? If it does, I understand and I used to be you as well.

I used to call myself the queen of networking until I realized that networking is very robotic. By definition, networking is the skill of exchanging professional experience between professionals In the hopes of developing professional or social contacts.

When you go to an event with the mindset that you are going there to network, you will probably formally approach people and overthink what you can or cannot talk to them about.

What I learned during my years of being the queen of networking is that I'm very good with small talk but I was not yet great at building relationships in a work environment. The best way to relate with someone is to relate to them in a personal way and not necessarily a professional way. There are many different ways that you can relate with someone personally without overstepping boundaries or being inappropriate.

When you start relationship-building instead of networking, you will find that you will make some friends at work and you will be able to bring your whole self to work, allowing you to be more authentic about who you are. This not only helps you but the people that you work with because they will be able to better celebrate you and work with you because they will know the real you.

In an earlier chapter, we talked about the importance of setting expectations with higher-level Executives when you start your new role. This is when you want to start building relationships. Not only do you want to set expectations and let them know where you see yourself in a year, but you also want to get to know them on a more personal level and also share about yourself. This will make it a lot easier to follow up and talk in future meetings because you will have things to talk about outside of work.

People love talking about themselves. As long as you are talking about something that they love, like their dog, cat, family member, celebration, or vacation, trust and believe that they will talk.

They may even talk for more than you probably want them to. But that's good because now you are having them open up to you and share a little bit more about their personal life which makes it a lot easier to build relationships. After all, now they see you as someone who relates to them or someone who cares about their life outside of work.

Here are some great conversation starters to build relationships with your coworkers.

- Who's your favorite singer?
- What's your favorite restaurant in the area?
- What are you reading right now?
- Who are some of your role models?
- What's the best book you've ever read?

- Where did you go to school?
- What's the best learning program you've gone to?
- What's the most interesting place you've ever traveled to?
- What's your favorite thing to do in your downtime?
- What do you do to de-stress?
- Tell me about your family.
- What's your favorite sport to watch (or play)?
- What was your very first job (and who was your very first boss)?
- Do you have any kids? How old are they?
- Do you have any vacation plans coming up?
- Find something relatable to what they are wearing, the decor in their office, or a gadget that they use to start a conversation

The other major part of relationship-building is the first impression. Within the first seven seconds of the meeting, people will have a solid impression of who you are.

Some research suggests that a tenth of a second is all it takes to start determining traits like trustworthiness.

So even if you're focused on building relationships, you have to make sure that you are making a great first impression to get to know them well.

First impressions have a huge impact on how people perceive you even while they are getting to know you. Here is a simple way to make a great first impression on anyone that you meet at work.

1. **Treat everyone like they were your boss.**

This may sound weird to you but the reason why it is important to treat everyone like they are your boss is so that you are not treating people differently according to their management level. This is very important because you will come across as someone who is naturally respectful and it will show others that you have integrity.

Sometimes people think that it is okay to treat seniors, managers, senior managers, directors, and partners with more respect than they treat their co-workers. However, they are only hurting themselves because if a senior manager sees you treating somebody else differently, they will automatically have a different impression of you.

Make it a habit to give everyone the respect they deserve because the way that you treat others will encourage them to treat you the same way.

Be willing to help everyone just like you are always willing to help your boss. Make sure that you are leading every conversation with gratitude and positivity and you will always make a great first impression on anyone you meet. This is especially important in case you are being talked about by a group of people that have different seniority levels. You do not want one person to express a different experience that they had from you compared to someone else because they are at different levels in the hierarchy. You should respect everyone, regardless of their level in the company.

Remember that your co-workers are also growing in their careers and will one day reach senior-level positions. You don't want how you treat them today to possibly affect your future. Also if you decide to leave this company you may one day need one of them to advocate for you for another opportunity in the marketplace. You never know when you will need someone so never burn any bridges or do something that will ruin your relationship with them in the future (unless absolutely necessary).

A huge part of being a leader is knowing how to serve others. Practice this by being willing to help out both your co-workers and senior-level management. Anytime you're able to help a co-worker you will make them remember that they're not alone and in turn that will make them feel very valued. This could pay off for you in the future because you never know how someone will be able to help you.

> **"I've learned that people will forget what you said, people will forget what you did, but people will never forget how you made them feel."**
>
> **Maya Angelo**

www.danielangounou.com

Reflection and Action Steps

What have you learned in this chapter?
How do you plan on implementing it?

_____
_____
_____
_____
_____
_____
_____
_____
_____
_____
_____
_____
_____
_____
_____
_____
_____

SECRET SEVEN

The Power Of Mentorship

Mentorship is powerful and can truly catapult your success. Check out this excerpt from a Buzzfeed article about the mentorship relationship between Christian Dior and Yves Saint Laurent, two very well known worldwide fashion brands.

"Christian Dior was one of the foremost designers of the 20th century, and the brand he started remains a fashion powerhouse to this day. In the final years of his life, Dior nurtured the talents of Yves Saint Laurent, the designer who would become his successor when he was just 21 years old.

Saint Laurent started working with Dior when he was still a teenager, and he spent two years "learning the secrets of haute couture from the master himself." In 1957, Dior told his business partner Jacques Rouet that, "Yves Saint Laurent is young, but he is an immense talent. In my last collection, I consider him to be the father of 34 out of the 180 designs. I think the time has come to reveal it to the press. My prestige won't suffer from it.

In 1986, Saint Laurent wrote of Dior, "He taught me the essentials. Then came other influences that, because he had taught me the essential, blended into this essential and found it to be a wonderful and prolific terrain, the necessary seeds that would allow me to assert myself, grow strong, blossom, and finally exude my own universe."

As you can see from this excerpt, Yves Saint Laurent is who they are today because they were mentored by Christian Dior. This is true for a lot of successful people today, including Mark Zuckerberg, Justin Bieber, Michael Jordan, and so many more.

All the celebrities boast about the joy of having a mentor and how their mentors gave them a head start toward success and helped them to avoid a lot of unnecessary mistakes and roadblocks. Finding a mentor during your career journey is something that you should consider. Most companies give you a career advisor or career mentor during your first few years at the firm. While it's great to leverage those mentors, I would also advise you to find someone outside of your workplace that can give you advice from a non-biased perspective.

The first step to doing this properly is finding your "why." Your "why" is your purpose, it is the reason why you wake up in the morning and why you choose to do the work that you do. Having a "why" frames the decisions you make for your career and life.

Your "why" can be described as your calling, your conviction, your mission statement, or a vision of your life and work. It can also be your core source of motivation, your reference point for all decisions and actions, who you are and what makes you productive, or the reason for your life's work or purpose.

If you still don't know what your why is after reading this, here is an exercise that you can do to figure out what it is. The goal is for your career to align to your why so that when you get up for work every morning it is with purpose and excitement because you are getting closer and closer to completing your life's mission.

That may sound overwhelming, however, this is how you start. This position may not be completely aligned with your why or what you feel is your life's mission, and this is where your mentor would come in. Before getting a mentor, it is helpful for you to understand where exactly you want to go and why you want to go there.

As a mentor, I have helped many people in their career as well as their entrepreneurship journeys to determine what their why is. Below is the exercise that I walk them through to figure this out.

- What are your values?
    - This is your personal code of conduct

2. What motivates you to work?
- What are you excited to work on without having to be told to do so or given an incentive to

3. What are your passions?
- These are things that you often cannot stop thinking about. Perhaps you are a go-to person for your family and friends when it comes to this topic.

4. What are your strengths?
- These are things that you are naturally very good at.

5. What are some things that tick you off? What are some problems in the world that you wish were not a thing?
- Try to be very specific here. An example for me is when people don't have the resources they need to accomplish the goals that they have.

6. Is there a problem or challenge that emotionally moves you to take action?

7. What kind of work would give you a sense of satisfaction or fulfillment?

8. What aspect of your career have you enjoyed across all your past work experiences?

9. What kind of work feels effortless to you, but drives your curiosity to learn more?

During this exercise try to ask yourself the question why until you get to the purest answer. This will allow you to see why you have a particular passion. Make sure to ask yourself why at least 4 times and at most 7 times to any of these questions.

After performing this exercise with clients of mine, a lot of people step into a more purposeful career and end up loving what they do. I hope this is the same experience for you!

Your first job in corporate does not have to be just a job, it can be the beginning of a blossoming career. If you start the journey correctly by understanding your why and pursuing things that are going to fulfill it, you are off to a perfect start! Find a mentor or coach that is already doing something similar to your why or has mentored others who have a similar "why." This will be very helpful in getting there successfully.

Corporate does not have to be a dreadful experience, as many would have you believe. The reason why most people do not like their experience in their nine-to-five jobs is that they are out of purpose and they're not living out their "why."

If you can't find someone that will mentor you

one-on-one just yet, find appropriate YouTube channels, blogs, podcasts, or social media pages that speak on topics related to your "why."

PERHAPS YOU WERE BORN FOR SUCH A TIME AS THIS

Esther 4:14

Reflection and Action Steps

What have you learned in this chapter?

How do you plan on implementing it?

_____

_____

_____

_____

_____

_____

_____

_____

_____

_____

_____

_____

_____

_____

_____

_____

_____

_____

_____

_____

BONUS SECRET
EIGHT

The Unfair Advantage

Have you ever heard of the statement that everything you have is everything you need? That statement holds very true especially when you take advantage of everything that you have access to.

For me, my unfair advantage is the Holy Spirit. The Holy Spirit is the Spirit of God that comes to live inside of anyone who accepts Jesus Christ as their lord and savior. The reason why I describe the Holy Spirit as an unfair advantage is that he knows all things, and he'll help you with all things if you want and allow him to.

When I started involving my faith in my career everything took off for me. I had several occasions where there were people who were not on my side, but I chose to trust God.

Earlier I mentioned how I had a really interesting director who ignored me for the first couple of months after meeting him. Because I had chosen to trust God with my career, I asked Him what I should do about this director. The Holy Spirit told me to pray for him. He told me to pray for his family and everything that concerns him. So that's what I did.

A day came when my director got really upset with me and asked me to give him a call. Before I gave him a call I went into the bathroom at work and I decided to speak in tongues, which means to pray in the spirit, allowing the

Holy Spirit to pray through me because honestly, I did not know what to pray at that moment. Well, after I got out of the bathroom and gave him a call we had one of the best conversations we had ever had in my whole time working with him at that point. It's like everything turned around and all of a sudden he had favor for me and wanted to uplift me and encourage me.

I knew that that was only by the power of the Holy Spirit.

I'm sharing this with you to let you know that you can do the same. You don't have to walk into your corporate journey by yourself. The one who created you is ready and able to help you at any time using your unfair advantage. When you choose to trust God with your job and your career as a whole, things become very different for you. You no longer get upset when someone is being rude to you because you know that as you're praying for them God is making all things work together for your good.

I have a video on my YouTube channel called "I prayed for my boss and this happened…" In that video, I talk about how things completely changed for me because of the prayer. That situation launched my career to a higher level than I ever thought possible. After that video, I received so many comments and emails on social media; messages about how other people started praying for their bosses and how it changed their careers for the better.

I want to invite you to join me in that challenge! Head to freegiftfromdaniela.com to join the challenge and make a lasting effect on your career!

And we know that all things work together for good to them that love God, to them who are called according to his purpose.
Romans 8:28

www.danielangounou.com

ONE LAST MESSAGE
Congratulations!

You just took a bold step towards getting lasting results in your career and self-development journey.

I am so proud of you for deciding to better yourself. I admire and respect you for being a leader and taking the right steps. This is how success is reached!

My mission with this book was to empower you and make a positive impact in your life by inspiring you to think differently and giving you practical steps to take.

Now you have another decision to make. You can choose to call this a good book and move on with your life, or you can choose to apply the strategies given to your life to see real results.

I have learned that no one has a time management problem but rather a decision making problem. People decide to stay up late, wake up late, eat bad food, and the list goes on.

So right now I challenge you to DECIDE to make a difference. DECIDE to be bold. And ONLY for those who have made that decision, reach out to me and tell me how this book helped you get to your desired results!

Take a picture of the front page of this book, tag me on Instagram @danielangounou and share with me what decision you made after this read!

"Carpe Diem! Seize The Day!"

~ Daniela Ngounou
Founder of The Professionals on Fire Network
www.freegiftfromdaniela.com

ACKNOWLEDGEMENTS

Through the years, many have shared ideas, mentoring and support that has impacted my life, each in a different way. It's impossible to thank everyone and I apologize for anyone not listed. Please know, that I appreciate you greatly.

Djessy Mampaka
Apostle Joshua Selman
Dr. Myles Munroe
Pastor Chris Oyakilome
Chad Gonzalez
Pastor Michael Todd
Andrew Wommack

James Malinchak
Nick and Megan Unsworth
Caleb Guilliams
Morgan Tracy

Jamie Campbell
Thompson Harner
Tulay Girard
John Moses
Maria Mosely
Laethitia Patadji

Donika Mooney
Marshall Crockett
Laurie Fleet
Colby Connor
Eric Butts
Peter Yobo
Frank M. Kobyluch Jr.
Al Zinkand
Adam Panfalone

www.danielangounou.com

Special **FREE** Bonus Gift for You

To help you to achieve more success, there are **FREE BONUS RESOURCES** for you at:

www.FreeGiftFromDaniela.com

- 3 in-depth training videos on how to excel in corporate

ABOUT DANIELA

Daniela Ngounou is an international speaker, best-selling author, and recognized as the #1 young professional success coach.

As the founder and CEO of Professionals on Fire, Daniela is on a mission to empower Young Professionals worldwide to excel in the areas of career, self-development, and faith

Daniela has a Youtube Channel with over 2 million views and is a community partner for the Girl Scouts organization.

Daniela Ngounou speaks for and engages audiences from 20-20,000, hosts workshops and training, as well as provides digital resources for the success of young professionals worldwide

www.danielangounou.com

Special **FREE** Bonus Gift for You

To help you to achieve more success, there are **FREE BONUS RESOURCES** for you at:

www.FreeGiftFromDaniela.com

- 3 in-depth training videos on how to excel in corporate

Made in the USA
Columbia, SC
16 September 2024

41870582R00065